There's the Hand and There's
the Arid Chair

*Translated from the Slovenian by
the author with:*

*Thomas Kane, Peter Richards,
Phillis Levin, Joshua Beckman,
Ana Jelnikar, Christopher Merrill,
Matthew Rohrer, Brian Henry,
and Anselm Hollo*

Edited by Thomas Kane

THERE'S THE HAND AND THERE'S THE ARID CHAIR

Tomaž Šalamun

COUNTERPATH PRESS

DENVER

2009

Counterpath Press
Denver, Colorado
www.counterpathpress.org

Compilation copyright © 2009 by Tomaž Šalamun
English translations copyright © 2009 by translators and/or author as
indicated in Translator Index on page 111.

Publication acknowledgments appear on pages 109–10, which
constitute a continuation of this copyright page.

Printed in the United States of America

Library of Congress Cataloging-in-Publication Data

Šalamun, Tomaž.
    [Poems. English. Selections]
    There's the hand and there's the arid chair / Tomaž Šalamun ;
translated from the Slovenian by the author with Thomas Kane . . .
[et al.] ; edited by Thomas Kane.
        p.   cm.
    Includes index.
    ISBN 978-1-933996-12-7 (pbk. : alk. paper)
    1. Šalamun, Tomaž—Translations into English.   I. Kane, Thomas.
II. Title.
PG1919.29.A5A2   2009
891.8'415—dc22

Cover collage by Brenda Iijima
Entrainment (detail), 2008
Collage with India ink

Distributed by Small Press Distribution (www.spdbooks.org)

Contents

I

II

III

IV

for Michael Thomas Taren

I

"Shoulder the sky, my lad, and drink your ale."

—A. E. Housman

Who Is Berkopec

Berkopec is a man who, when I was almost fourteen years
old and my father for the first time
took me with him on the plane to watch the earth,
passed by in the park in Sarajevo when
my father slept on a bench and I watched and named him
Berkopec.

Beauty of Man

Beauty of man is the furthest history.
We have pressed peaches.
Nobody is coming out from little huts.
We know, squeezed.

The building eroded into its horizon.
I didn't propel anything that wouldn't go to pasture.
I kneaded round kerchiefs inscribed above the fresco.
The one who doesn't pledge the horizon,
how would he pay for it?

The tones don't know what apples are.
The defense knows.
It bites the serene one.

The great blindness tells iodine:
dress up, stay.
Your little barrel is the arrogant's clay.
And: on the white sand the grass grows.

I'm from tonight.

Amtrak, New York—Montreal,
January 24, 1974

First I shivered like a switch on water,
because of the "chain of accidents." The second
thought was: I'd like to be at least as systematic

as Swedenborg. Was the frame clear?
I accepted it, even if all layers of my body
didn't yet go through the groove?

Immediately after—I've seen it in a flash—
the angels were censorship and fog, only
a field of space that drags you to the middle.

They paled quickly and glued themselves into a lump.
I sensed physical arms, they gently seized me
under my armpits. The air droned. But not

as if the hard body would pierce through it, instead as if
someone would drag me through milk. They all
expected me, although my physical presence

was noticed only gradually. First the old ones,
then those of middle age, then the young.
As if someone widened their visual field

with the rheostat. Some of them
let me know they were carrots; their skin
was scratched off, already on the earth. Some of them

felt vividly that they only had to go headfirst
through the waterfall. I was interested in
who selected them to be here, but my thought

died away, they stopped it, I couldn't utter it.
Stopping it was like a drop falling in water,
expanding the water in circles. Clear waves, I traveled

with them. A compact lump (above my head)
licked me and flooded me with pathos and delight.
A beam (a cone) coming from this lump

tore me apart, diffused me horizontally,
though I was the same. I knew:
they have other sources, more powerful,

calmer. I noticed seemingly connected clothes.
Veils (clouds) in the attitude of breasts.
I didn't walk on the ground but on something

hanged, it looked like ice or glass
(optically) although I sensed everything:
the moss, the parquet, the grass, the asphalt (green!).

I didn't see this with my eyes but with my skin,
as if the skin was looking. At the same time I read
Haiku, I. G. Plamen, for awhile *The Village*

Voice. I was on the train, looked through the
window, read again. I understood everything all at
once. The language is "articulated" and "mute" at the

same time, it happens in tepid flashes. Accidents are
the humus. As if ping-pong balls would fly from
all directions at the same time to massage you.

The Shirt

To tear the shirt and clean the soul is crucial.
What makes language is accidental.
To burn Joan of Arc.
Joan of Arc had a beak.
Rakes stung the bees.
There were no power plants back then.
Waters rolled freely.
Fields, bulks of soldiers difficult to scan, lances.
Master Eckhart uses the word
detached exactly as Ljubljana's
teenager uses the word *odbit*.
Out of freedom I would lick them.
Out of freedom I lick them.
They both point with their fingers: there!
There, it strangles, roots out, and God produces
a waterfall over your head.
You lean a ladder against the air and it does not fall.
With pins you pump out the air.
The earthworm is gifted.
It goes to the ear's little hair.
He winds around the trunk
like the tree in paradise winds around the serpent.

Will You Die?

Masses smelled holes in a box.
They opened their own reserves.

They used glue.
Masses compared a carousel with

a drum, a horizontal arc
with a ventilator-propeller.

The bird's skin, that the bird cannot eat, itches.
A man sweats, he's near a computer,

he eats soup. Young painters drop
their prizes. I'll kiss you in

public. I'll kiss you in the museum
and look at your sphinxlike

crumbs. To our sorrow, to my sorrow,
to your sorrow, the white, terrible horizon.

The Body of Giordano Bruno

Light brown bug, Queen Mother,
your pellet of shit is dangerous.
That's why they burned him. He flooded
the Protestant imagination and
Catholic images spilled over the brim.
Sigillum sigillorum sleeps, unless
touched by the Mother of the Pyramids.
All my life I've been writing the seals.
I'm the water that flows through his body.
The stake tames the muscles. The virus
in the computers, which prevents the seal
from running, is the secular
illness inherited from the defense.

The light brown bug, Queen Mother,
you, who have access to the iron
hooks hanging like the tools of countenance
in the mouth, not even a path through
the field to Menorca, a stone wall
that would have nothing to do with this.
Reading the seals abolishes matter.
Andro has to wiggle as he climbs.
In a couple of hours both of us are worn out,
then we loll between the walls, discussing
for the next day the droppings of the sacred bees.

The light withdraws into silence,
The Holy Spirit gives a cap to the void,
air to the fish, suddenly connecting,
from one point to another, the view of the horizon,
you can see the legs of birds, a coffin

in an envelope with velvet
springs. They spread tons of heraldic
kitsch, attentive as milk.

The grass is authentic.
Light brown bug, Queen Mother,
blood drips from the chickens on the trains,
from a lunch box prepared with
love at the turn of the century,
brown shit, fig jam,
trenches in a desert, where the axis rotates on its points,
lances and dustmen sweeping the garbage into a pile.

Flowers

My mother was a diamond-merchant's daughter.
She swam across a corona.
We bought a cow to pasture.
We caressed servant girls in the Simplon Express.

She had to learn how to cook.
My great-grandmother was able
to make everything except shoes.
We carried bark.

Our baron great-granduncles
visited us once a year.
Exactly where Nabokov peed
in his pants and a few meters away
from where uncle Guido
saw the shark snap his lover's thigh.

When I saw a violinist for the first time,
somebody pushed me into a cactus.

I didn't understand what the bows were,
why they rubbed on the strings.

Blossom and Blood

I'm the fruit whose skin breaks,
a container grabbed with a crane.
Gulls are bloodthirsty and hungry.
Their plucked feathers descend
as I climb. Booms, silky booms
in the frozen boat's throat, between
the sliding rusty doors of the tanker.
What do I do here if my seal breaks?
How should I grease my black and blue shoulders?
Hey, little stoker, I squeezed your head
under the ceiling when I started to breathe.
Your limbs, smashed on brown metal,
cannot be washed away. A mosquito is caught in oil.
They nail the box Illyria on a stick
and when the lid is pressed to the ceiling
where should it go if not inside? You resemble
an old fly's turd looking partly gray on a light bulb.
Shall we throw spears? I don't have a tool.
And the huge trunk with a pulley, coming closer,
owns nothing. I'm shifted around.
Machines are putting me on the other dock.
And from there a train through
dark tunnels and damp gorges
or in the sun, sun among wheat spikes,
an hour before the arch goes out and the lights
of cars and houses ignite. How should I
remember you, little stoker? I'm almost
unloaded. Only a lintel or two,
only a distance traveled on foot and then
that closeness with the heart shown by your

hand. A span. A span. You slap wood
as if a piano, you measure the tone.
Such sweet sounds Pythagoras takes.

Dark Glasses

My called number is not a purse.
My heart belongs to daddy.
A myrtle tree and eyes: I take a muff.
To uproot Buñuel's eye: a fountain. Your
neck grew longer. Deep, the water is
ice cold. Sarah swims in the well.
She wears her wedding dress.
Wet as butterflies. She is preserved.
She's dead, already thirty years.
I always objected to those who
wrote about food. We had to march
kilometers passing by Dutch
paintings. I plucked them.
I opened the earth. Smelled them
above the abysses and drowned them.

The deer braids the turtle.
But a sketch of a braid, because the turtle has no hair.
Oh, you can't have everything.
The cow can't harvest corn.

To Świetlicki

In the same ambience Tito sang:

Canoe, canoe
why do you row,
who will you still rub in the snow,
who do you really need?

Already Świetlicki came rushing,
otherwise impossible to pull out of
Poland.

This guy believes in his throat and his sewing pants.
Butterflies are oystermen.
Little ducks have little skin on their fins.

Terrible whiteness of diminutives,
do you feel: you give—I give?

If you enlarge the bumblebees' eyes,
hornets commit suicide.
They, the ridiculous ones, drone on like a gang.

Virgil

All this blinking, gurgling, sweet stinking,

decadent, soul-racked sorrel—

the love of decanting,

snails put into the mouth, glued to the heart,

this stupor of marshland.

Daze of swamps, moisture swollen

from damp and ardor, an overcraved soul

pressed by cognition.

I was not tugged from Ljubljana,

like you Virgil, from the province by

Caesar.

I move compactly,

fast, *il duca.*

Without gloom and vaporizing.

Your bad luck was:

barbarians were outside,

Rome was empty.

My good luck is:

barbarians are inside the skin of America.

I'm a Hittite.

I don't pay because I'm high.

God's Teethridge

Let's say ants with long eyelashes
jumped out of a begonia. Such eyelashes
don't exist. There're no ants that would jump

out of a begonia. The sole start is pressed.
Ants are always composed of brown hills.
They're undercut and you don't know

how the bowels, pipes, highways—
how surely they use them at the decanting—
splash into the second half of the axis. At

the passages one can feel the ridge of God's
teeth. At times they injected workers
into the concrete. One worker: he staggered.

The helmet and the body under the helmet are
filled with the wet mane. There're gas sticks
in the cathedrals. The refraction of light hammered

into the vitrage. Then, boxers with polished-off
flesh were not on the scene, not yet. Margaritas will be
swirled. Doves jump on the shelf. The wings,

they need them in the open. The Holy Spirit sags
into the basalt. God's teethridge cannot hide it.
You can't dissolve the rainbow with saliva.

Sardines

Chaos squats. The mushroom sifts
feet. The scarf breaks the neck. Rabbits jump
over fences and break peanuts. Alessandro
Carissimo di Parma for the hand of
Christ. Don't laugh into my eyebrows,
my eyebrows are dramas. They teach
better than the freckle. The iron from Lisbon's
elevator broke my step. The man
makes the butcher smaller and keeps
making him even smaller. The stake—
the tooth of its own water—stomps.
It moves. It high tides. Jump on the divan.
There's a gun above the divan. *Siamo
vicinissimi.* Under the divan there's a sword.

The Right of the Elephant's Bone

Those wounded by Šalamun have their own
club,

with their eye's right
and their own public transportation.

The wise ones make progress.
To give to eat.

The pig's paw on the loam behaves
differently than the pig's paw

on the wet cement.
Calm the plant.

Mutilate the daffodil.
Count the drawers and entrances.

Live in the time of
abrupt needs.

Better Drunk than Old

Look how nice you combed yourself. Leaves'
rituals flash in the magnanimity. The joy is in
the cheerfulness. Tautologies are no more for

castigation. The little spheres, as if when you make
children. They're taken from what was already
there. The mountain grows out of love, the hills

grow out of a snake. And if more millipedes grow,
food for the eyes is automatic. By not being
sanded, they flash. Hammers, sofa beds,

worms, hikers heading toward Mount Nanos,
why then does the air not hit the air? It does.
The world of the next millennium will be

rich and calm. We're only now getting used to
delights, not to be torn apart. Look: the pin
and the elephant, my sand in the cup

and the Gobi desert, these are the distances
between love and love. The body has
to accustom itself, knowing already what's

eternal. But what we can take with us, we have
to learn. Young people have their hopes
still glued to the tassel. They rarely even

know what they have under the birch tree.
We'll melt binding the feet of Chinese women,
there will be no return into the dark throat.

The grace will be infinite, juicy, divisible
and indivisible, and what was once
given will be the noncombustible well.

Moro

The heraldry is a warm, round wagon for
milk. Heartbeats blow over lakes.

Houses, castles, dots beam upon the afternoon of Sonia
Wetchera. Years decay, plums get dry.

A little in the night, a little in the milfoil.
Gestures and sheep and spheres burn. They

wet themselves with saliva in the sun. We bend plastic bottles.
Animals make us happy. Here, what is lacking in the wood.

O core of pine trees!
An accordionist and Gongora. A tinsmith, a returned

emigrant, a pilgrim. The Leopardi's skin. Iodine in
dots. The smoke above the roofs in

conflagration. The meaty breast. The frisk tissue.
Did you paint the stucco work, you, Dalmatian girl?

The Suns

What you insert into love is paid for.
The whole oil tanker of scales and cabbage heads.
All the fish scales in the world cannot satiate
the 300,000-ton oil tanker.
Helium from the tree is empty.
Flour is the only starting point.
With what do you cement fugues?
In the mouth, in the nostrils, in the ears, don't you burst?
The dove takes on a blue color in flight.
The whiteness of the dress hurts.
Shall I take off your skin as well?
Where does it lacerate?
What's in cradles and valleys?
Where are your little sisters?
Can I nail myself into eternity without pain?
Where is your penholder?
The little stool, does it hurt?
Who rivets the screaming ears of birds?
Lie down, little doe!
Rest in peace and mew.
It's warm in the snow.
Where is my voice?
Without pain you return to your drawing room.
Everything is in place.
Vases. Leather. Roses.

Now Karen and Richard's House

You, who caressed my snout and paw,
I need you.
Isn't a meter stack of white argil
the heart's hand?
Drink mass for the dead.
Gulp Muddy Lake.
High priests form wings, they draw
rhombs, only so both of us might decant.
If we can absorb and dissolve them.
In the night, students brought to the pedestal:
nails,
the skin of a rabbit's mouth,
the tiny bell from the Alps,
Auden (who was a friend of the deceased principal),
strange scales,
strange dust,
violet blossoms.
They sang all night long, moved
silently in the forest.

II

"A fleece had been made out of all the beauty that had been flung from the knot's egress." . . . "Your once plumb hag grass sinks to a sinew that the child might chew on as a changeling root or a heart not yet awoken in a chest."

—Michael Thomas Taren

If Here

If I don't think it here, I don't anywhere.
To which conclusions should I come?
To wounds? Isn't it better to lick wounds

than to heal them, as they would not
drain away? Therefore I throw brushwood
on them and burn them. Fire, smoke, twigs,

as long as they blaze and even then no more.
A bit how we hide, a bit how we put on
our T-shirt, how we take it off, a bit how we

repeat the gesture so to be hidden completely.
We're stripped and vulnerable. Shall I
offer you my heart? What will you do with it?

Will you eat it up with a crunching noise?
And where will it be then? Isn't it better to burn it
for good? To watch how it smokes and becomes

blue? Splash! And the oar wrenches up from
the depths, that's what I wanted, again it
falls right-angled, it pulls, draws, muscles strain,

the boat flies. The boat has to be light if it should
fly and the excellent rower, twice removed
cousin from Bled, I don't know who bleaches

his hair, he or his younger rower. I don't know
what their name is, if they're related at all.
I think the relative doesn't have trophies.

Those with trophies are not relatives. And so
I amuse myself with water, with splashing and
ticking, because what lovely ticks relieve pain.

Creatures roll on
green branches
of beech tree.
They sleep on a roof
made of straw in my
head. Waves of crying
silk rustle behind their
things.
Sometimes they have the shape
of a chicken or
a priest's huge red
wadded heart.
House dwarves
bow to them. Pan
in the middle of a garden
lifts a goblet. Storks
also read this as a fantastic
sign, and a neighbor runs up to a well,
a bit nervous. She whispers:
again he sups on nurslings,
again he crushes gold dung.

Green Catastrophe in Trieste, 1910

Good morning, grashopper!
I imagined you with long golden
hair worn loose, but you're
nothing but a pair of long green legs.
So you're green, not blonde.
No big deal.
Pastures are green,
angels on some old masters'
oils are green, and horsemen are bluish green.
When crystals are flooded with green
we hear noise and the rattle
from the quarrel with white.
Laura's black eyes,
her golden hair,
became the green of Vaucluse.
Mint is green.
Mentula of Catullus, what is your color?
Here I interfere in the vision of my grandmother,
green for her fortold catastrophe.
All ladies who, from their boxes,
through their opera glasses circled with pearl,
peered out at the catastrophe, had seen
flogiston's green flame blazing from its curls.
ACID?
Was it really curly?
Didn't you tell us Mme Helena Petrovna
Blavatskaya seduced you all?

Zebra's Body

With all the keys, I rattled, I started
to climb the hill. Flies were swallowed by

a siphon. The darkness was hard like a
vigorously cooked egg. The others skied.

I pulled my lasso out of the snow. Soft bodies
were bumping into aluminum foil. We were

sitting at the table, eating. A fisherman who
didn't clean his net, a chimney sweep,

dining, stood near the fireplace. The laugh
has a form of kasha. Having no form, it

smolders. The wind started to move above
pine trees. We, all of us at the dinner, with

all of our towers, are luckily worth more than
a sled in the night, opening itself like a blue box.

The Detour across Delaware

Inebriating. We're inebriating. Seasons are
clay windows, we climb through them
all radiant. We count push-ups.

With yoga the leg might go into the mouth.
I noticed you're trimmed.
The most interesting to me was

the epic route that remained only in segments,
as dead bricks. Still, the underworld
knows what it knows. It knows

how to stuff the dead animals, how
to paint the upper layer of the little hands.
Don't cry because they

licked it. Only time gets exhausted from
rubbing. We're children in grain,
all three with hair. Beauty

corrodes our face. I take Yahweh's
prick and write with it,
because it lay on the table, sun!

The Little Plaque Is Formed by Fire and God

The left-handed man's mouthful
is worth more than the lifting of roofs.
Love has a head and flesh.

Wet, injured persons march across a ravine.
Who has a head and nostrils?
To believe and to open bread with the mouth.

To bet on Gypsies.
The sun would donate to both of them,
to the pale one and the abandoned one.

On the fish there's flour.
A black nettle.
In clay there are two erect soldiers.

Both of them drink.
A mare, mixed with bread and salt,
falls upon all four sockets.

O skier, do you still remember?
Burda must be below raspberries.
A whistle saddles a tugboat

and beats on the spire. If you break
through him with a probe you see the sky.
If you dress him in a coat you see fairytales.

The Hanging on the Flagpole

Fils d'un pompier et grand voyageur,
he thought he'd become a butterfly, but he became
Hiroshige. And the hazelnut falling from

the hazel tree, does it touch
the window? The furs lie on the field
and don't catch a cold. The wheel rotates.

You're a blockhead, you have vermin in your
heart. Rough ruffians sink into stars.
I hang in juice and kiss the firmament.

I think the fairytale.
I make the fairytale.
I shield the fairytale.

I find shelter under the bright sky.
Little hens—you're barefoot.
I hatch every third egg.

Little hens—they cut off your antlers,
they didn't cut them off of snails.
The fable, if it tangles in the throat,

reminds me of the entirely wet garden net.
The wall gets through the silent files of people
by itself, it bends them and lightens them.

Leonardo's Horse

Do you sink in eiderdowns, sheets, night bonbons?
What about the Sava River? Does it still run? Are you
playful near shutters? To take down his skirt. The ancient

dream was carried out. And to flip around the fish
on marks of reconciliation. The thorns' crown of golden
wires. Who doesn't perforate the surface, the cricket

or the loam? The praying mantis drowns like a heavy rat.
Only the proboscis shines. And the water beetle. He doesn't
perforate the surface. In the dusk, not seeing, he

still believes in elasticity. To collect water in a pout?
Is it possible? To draw the mountain, all punctured,
to show how the cake fries in it? To make a big bathtub

out of tufa? To plaster with silt the syringe of teledynamic
powers? All this is possible. We can take away a heart.
Horses—seven hundred thirteen—can be lifted above

the planks. From the air they can lower a milk pail and
peanuts, soft and hard figs, to wait, to brighten the rain,
the place, with different rebounds and names.

———

you'll be surprised but it isn't so
very tall trees do not provide a lot of shade
a lot of shade is found under the short, fat trees

The Sword

I
swing
the
sword
so
it
covers
the
whole
page
and
to
be
in
the
sword
is
delight
and
to
hiss
with
the
sword
is
delight.

The Bucolic One

We draw planks near. Pooh, quicklime, dry skin,
it all goes behind nails. You pump the balloon.
The basket, markers, the helmet made of leather

and goggles. Neat. Will you jump from the balloon
to the trampoline made only for body weight?
Gravitation isn't coupons you can tear off,

all of them at once. You'd kill yourself, tearing
them off all at once. Lungs widen. The space
changes, you stand up and sing, sing and sing,

the space becomes blue, your hair stands up,
you undress and dance, it sprinkles, brains literally
spray and you go into the belly of a spider,

settle there, pick up a broom in the first moment,
clean a bit in this huge sphere, then see the walls
blot what is under the broom, and again

you stand up and sing, you swing in a sort of
live sand. The walls start to drip. You don't hit
the keys anymore. The scribe looks over his shoulder

and asks: shouldn't we stop for today, as it seems
the spider's belly will burst? And where shall we
go then? On the paper? With all this birth water?

———

Who lives in the error that color is culture
and fish is nature will get sober.
The trees are hair on the skin planted by us.

———

In front of the eyes it is bright, behind the eyes it is dark.
Turning the head is a total utopia.

———

Your hands burned to let you be without hands.
You will be charged for switching rails and killing people.

———

The bird gets scared,
the worm gets scared,
the brain covers up.

Movements

You went to heaven, Sir,
forgetting your legs. Should we bury them?

My legs are rose-pink and they're no good for a wafer.

———

Wanderer, the moon has its own saying:

I would pour over your face with a bucket so
the water would flow onto your clothes.

———

Biscuits stick to each other differently than peanuts.
He started to nibble at my girlfriend.

———

I remember the clear day and
the glimmering of frozen gutters.
We muse over those we love.
We evaporate their most tender memories like a roast meat.

You don't move upon love,
you move upon a territory.

———

Then I liked him.
I stopped to shift you.

Ants, like Somalian women,
have jugs on their heads.

———

Doesn't the happiness of falling into mud
have its share of grey color?
Halt yourself. Somebody walks the Franciscan street.
My body is my permanent possession.

———

Heaven was conceived with a knife.
In the hut there were no corn grains.
If you slip your little hoop around a harbor seal
will it pour liquid on the banks?
Everything in Korea is green,
fresh mountain people kneaded into a town.

———

Maybe there's an army in the horses.
Maybe someone spins a cymbal in his belly.
In Aquilea the sand lays on the ground.
Night is in your head.
The space reserved for a terrible long sleep.

Tell me.
I fried a carriage.
You listen because I tame beasts.

These Are the Islands

These are the islands of Vis and Hvar!
Two lullabies above the complexion of black golden
Saturns. Hills, charred long ago during
the bleating of sheep and lambs,
during the elliptical carriers of fire,
and rain forcing its way between
branches, without noticing the leaves, without
drinking them.
For years I felt that orange shovel.
I know what I say,
lynx, I had you followed by my
officers equipped with binoculars.
Listen: you should only care for your
outer appearance, for your black lacquered
boots and the precise straight movements of your
dealings. Everything else
will be brought to you on a platter,
given. When the arc is black—
thunder—when it is clearest and smoothest like
cobalt, when the sky is a stitched up
blanket of enamel tiles,
how will I know!
It was already the sixteenth day of my sailing
with muscles, with my almost crushed
ebony and rusty sunsets,
so the crew tottered already up to the crest,
on their backs. The illegals had gone.
They fled with their tailored objects.
The sea was so warm that it sizzled like
the lamentations of those surrounded and

crammed into a bag. Who (I knew it)
could endure without towers—
constructions ordained
by ancestors. Does the mast not
crack when no more grease remains
disarmed in the boiling mouth of the sun?
How then did I get to the millet, I, a horse?
Wow!
Beams were scorched, God himself could not
tell apart the bleating from the victims.
But then again he might,
that is why I go on with my story.
The shattered had quickly sifted
the wheat from the chaff and to the sound of a whistle.
Watch out! I still insist on formalities!
It caught fire by itself.
The sea, which had for centuries floated as though
inside a dark wine bottle, took on
the charm. And now it no longer matters: the squeaking of
the winch, hydrofoil, the Lehman collection,
dew on an avocado, a fruit that presently
withstands the gravel of the Alps,
jokes that all people know,
but among the animals only the religious beasts,
the only true mathematicians of nobility.
Where then could it be
moored, my triple-masted boat?

———

Mountains, all their life on the spot,
crush the distance.

Space is only for one color: white.

———

There are no bonds for the seventh day.

———

Who has the same name as the other
and who has the same name as you
misses electricity.
Every mythological status is bread.
To the earth, which is hollow
and surrounded by walls of carpets of grass,
we will cut the artery, so the air will rush out.
Let giants eat the sandwich.

Nice Hat. Thanks.

Little burnt villages. Heavy drinkers.
Incredible! Such is my influence:
We're ducks.
I took the distribution and the title from Joshua.
Arms are a genuine feeling.
These are our mouths and palms.
Frogs are resoled.
O God, how near we are to each other.
I lick God's mind and roll over like a turtle.
The swallow's dome has pity and destroys.
Heaps of sand. Mothers, mothers.
The enemy is tortured and juts out.
Mommy carries the chapter.

Frontier

But you know, suffering also decays
and remains dust.
The frontier is my living body.
When a peasant burns his partridges.
It grabs. It grabs.
The earth should clean itself.
It is burning up dry grass.
It removes wood and sells it.
Children bring it milk on handcarts
so the co-op pays him for gas.
It exults in rain, when it's needed.
And sunshine, when it suits the grain, not him.
It's free.

How the Hills

How the hills
glow. Hunters
wipe

their sweat.
The bloom is
the harbor of the bees,

but they
do not endure
in this position.

They soar
and fly away.
I am heading

for the car,
the sun
is going down.

It is time
to drive
home,

we will eat
and go
to bed.

III

"This circle," he said, "which the blotter has made
into a point invaded by night is God."

—Edmond Jabès

Eternity is
cruel and crystal.
It ruins

everything alive.
It replaces people and
loves and does not

open
the well. With your hand
you dust a glass,

you do not
break it. Let every
love

die as
a man does. Death
protects us.

A Bathed Newborn

The lifetime annuity broadens like a stain.
I live on cranberries and raspberries.

Three Flies

Three flies—the sun wakes them
on the white, brightened wall—jump like
the hands of the girl, wrapping up a bunch
of flowers. They remind me of
the knife-thrower's hands, playing with five
in the air. Is the quantity limited?
Grab, don't think. Weigh on
me. I'll escape you like water yet. I'll
press you like ice if you sizzle too much.
Look at the shades on the white wall.
Three trees have the new
cedar scion. From the angle of
the cube. And if you watch more closely,
from the gutter spout.

ACI

I'm a primordial being with a hidden fly,
my eyes are in the tunnel.

The tongues of various bells surround me,
I hang in the drawer.

I skate from dawn to dusk.
Birds, for me, are like boats.

Sometimes I think I have wooden marrow.
Mistake! I only have red shoes.

Firs and spruces wear manes.
Manes for me.

I am the circle of immunity
broken off, voilà, it's gone.

As what breaks off comes back
as a panther.

Black Sun

Inferno happened when Dante explained to us how
he functions sexually.
Before then, it did not exist.
And Petrarch.
Who like a green dog on four wet, dark-green legs
sniffs Vaucluse and touches his clothes.
He thinks about the the books his father
burnt, not about Laura.
It has to do with the race.
Who is faster.
God with his sand or we with our tongue.
Sand is the tongue of fire.
Tongue is the fire of sand.
Fire is the sand of God.
I'm falling.
I fall like an oak doomed to die, and also
women want to be more than metaphor.
With their moist, round, soft skin, with their
drunken scent of warm mushrooms they drive me insane.
Walls of hell, why do you stagger.
I miss the smell of burnt flesh.
Nature makes me tired.
It tires me so terribly that I sink in a cave.
Stars move apart.
I am the Sun.
With no air.
Fake fire falls upon the children's black hair,
advancing into their hearts so they burst like buckles.
Their mouths yawn open as if they were mummies.

They rave in benediction, they gargle my
name as I get dressed.
When I adjust my collar in front of him—the mirror—
everything is already late.

You did not snow me in.
By my own choice I went under.
Defenses collapsed, my friend.
Woods and fields resting.

Welded by too much of you hammering
I dissolve.
I sweep myself off because I love.
Here too: loss is the only delight.

Benito Mussolini Has His Fingers in His Pants

The sheatfish started to swim. *Adieu*, sheatfish, *Adieu!*
As the white of an egg bursts when you throw him
into a black nettle. The cardinal who looked at me
through the paper called to me with guile. Mares—
more and more scarce—felt their way.
I know what I transport. I transport
cakes. With my boot I move the hill. From
Beelzebub—he doesn't have styropore in his voice—
drips *merci, merci*. My machine performs itself: a pullet
and at the same time, a deal board and a pullet.
Moss was lodged and rustled. Pearls were
entangled in a carburetor. A whale lives in the
countryside. Its eyes are supported by timberworks.
Its eyelids are the mortar of unborn sons.

———

You *are* my angel.
A mouth dusted with chalk.
I'm a servant of the ritual.
The untouched.

White mushrooms on a white field.
In a horizon of fire.

I am walking on the gold dust.

Warning the Sphinx

White, white night, burn for me the grass.

I swing in the angle between the white unslaked lime, the white

unslaked lime.

My lover is afraid he won't be a guy any more.

———

The soul on the barge.

The hand on the shallow ground.

———

The little man with the little yellow paw will

wet the white cube and the feathers that I

stick into my hair.

———

The stomach, the white ham.

The father, the edge of flesh.

The rams slept on bags turning into blue

stones.

———

In reserve,

by the head's small moves,

I discover an earth that glaciers have torn apart.
I retrieve the greenness to Paros.

———

Will you come, Terrible one?

I prepared you mead and rags from the earth's stubble.

We'll need to sink the yellow boats.

Come.

———

To slobber on Job with grey velvet.

———

Through the Pentagram's window

marches the cute little boy.

His fingers have dug into the sky,

as if glued on by honey.

———

Raise the hat!

You too, Maximal Participation, Azure

Plunderer.

———

I'm a log.

I'm Pont.

I'm your bone of flesh.
Therefore you testify for the Face.

The Piece of Earwig, Fainted in Amber,
Can Plug the Crime Out

Numbed, we counted ourselves into the thickness of the earth,
pieces of earwig fainting into the amber.

The wet deck, *vzglavka*, why do you give me light?
O, my touched one. Children on the street creak, decanted for
noise.

I know I stood on stamps.
We washed mountains, we boxed between blotting papers.

A lot of eaten-up things here, nothing funny.
Don't let your foot be eaten up, you'll need it.

The concave tradition failed.
You put in the piss, you pump it out and mitigate

factions. Let down shutters. In hell there're shutters.
I imagine a sphere-thrower, kin to divinity.

Gombrowicz is a dark fiasco. At the end
a lemon was stuck to him.

On the grass, on its own, the monkey brise-soleil is lying.
On the grass, on its own, the monkey brise-soleil is lying.

New Moon

When I stared, to catch sight of a bird,
a litter enlarged sixty times, a piece
of brown-red, slowly moving fig

marmalade. When I looked round
to see if some chicken from a freezer
was put in a cardboard box,

in the compartment above my head. Who
dug up my crumbs? Who sharpened my ice?
sometimes a rowan simply washes ashore.

I have neither rakes nor hayforks,
all my hippopotamuses died. And the sun
shines behind golden ears. The sun shines

behind golden ears even when they're moved
by oxen. Then I watch the location. Very near
where the Romans project it, it subsides—

as if it went for small, low hills but in
fact it is about solid land, about the Karst.
Now who cares, if from a window you threw every daisy.

Sand and Rollerblades

Menelaus carves out a cube, supports the
cube. Birds have scythes with whetstones.
A tube bends like a pipe of lungs and a driver

stands upright. Biscuits are whiter at the turn of
centuries. In slush, in dew, in cotton pads. Censuses
are like horizontal bars, everybody can do them

but if only the timetable is confirmed again and
again. A bird has a salty eye. It doesn't give up during
exams. It walks on carpets, it melts windows.

The earth is a pin. The hills are dashes and poems.
Musical scores don't climb like animal patents,
all of them are the same, from windpipe to

Christ. Will he embrace the whole shebang? Are
crossing guards also in a rice meat pie? When it
jabs with a beak? When he cuts the link,

cuts the pace? With his palms he makes rolls.
They're baked by radiation. There's neither the
back, nor the bones, nor the skin. The

arms lift themselves and vanish like
railroad gates. Look at the type of gratitude
and the nature of sheltering. The sensation

of sinking no longer exists. The sensation
collapsed. There's the sensation that ice will
endure, that violets will grow green upon the ice.

Are More Mysterious than My Rain

We'll be no more.
We'll be gone,
asking for milk.

We'll remember
brambleberries and the wild
race over the hill:

"Who comes
first to lunch gets
a special treat and a ride

in the boat.
A flamingo—
the names of Mary of the Rose."

Afternoon, at the Table,
above the Underworld

I sewed pants,
I sewed pants and tore off the thread with my teeth.
I chucked white spheres of loam
into your hall, from inside, among flowers.

Virgil started to blossom, he lies in the mud.
There are leather dumbbells and a horizontal bar
glistening with sneaky light, like yours,
as if guard dogs would attack you.

No one has seen a man here since
the last castaway—rolled up like a sheet
of paper around an empty gas can—
surrendered to the glory of ghosts.

I sewed pants and blinded you in an instant.
Pay attention, you should know what you eat.
Salomé, Salomé, your head is still on a wire,
earthy and watery and splattered

all over with wild turkey feathers.
Do you remember how I dislocated your head?
It was too cream-colored, garish,
with no flavor, it had no flavor.

God grant that we would get it
in the underworld! I sewed pants
and let my foot down to you. There.
To swim. Alone. To leap.

To go mad alone, it has no experience being
torn off. It recognizes nothing, like you.

If you make it a pin, it falls.
If you press it into thick mud,

it is afraid to be in the swamp.
But it's not in the swamp, blockhead,
you're in it, alone, without it.
The foot is in the warmish place, secure.

Nakedness of the Wall

Who swung his arm
to peel the cave?
At night there is a white cellar,
a god who hurts.
A god who lies down
on the sea and chokes the waves.
They crack like mountain flint stones,
totally stiffened. They brake like
dust under the feet of dust.

My Brides Are of Gobelin

Would you be able to call upon your shoulder and give it to the Society of Anti-fascist Women?

Kittens would then lick milk. A random traveler would kick the inside wall of an elevator.

We forgot about plants. We watch them through the glass. I breathe as if the mountain is

a huge tire, as if the propellers and Noguchi's lamps are also blessed. Now I pushed my knee

through the fence, I don't identify with Voznesensky (a heart struck him) but with

hummingbirds and a butcher shop. With sewing cotton measured by ells and a chirping bird: here I

fly, here I fly, take me down to this hut. As Vasilij made his hands dry, no wonder he held them up.

I Wouldn't Husk the Concert to Myself
Even in My Dreams

Third Barabbas, build the wall.
To third Barabbas: the wall will crumble.
The sun fell on your neck,

through the sheet of glass in your car.
We'll die and bathe ourselves in thatch.
With pleasure, I've heard the fighting stall,

knocked down so the sun will still
turn. Tons sweep to the earth.
Being anonymous, I have wet sleeves.

We dragged the idiot pilot to the rock
and dried his hair. Do you want me to save
your life? Would you trust a deformity

sustained with beams and dressed
in an impermeable fold? I don't know.
I don't even know if I'd shun a puddle.

Toledo gives me an eyelash for my
eye. I'd shuck peas. It wears a silky plastic
coat. I believe I'll dry out like a log.

Madreperla, Gifted to the Scythians

Everyone valued as twice the quadrant
will die lined up with wood.
I find shelter from the rain below breath,
not in the breath.
In the breath I hammer nails.

Inside, deeply inside, there were
gray mattresses with sprinkled blood.
We used to carry clods of pigs to the fence,
laying them into the abyss when
trains passed by, not to be
heard too much.

Mangalia

I'm a lackey's brother,
a fish's flock of sacred marasca.
I'm the internal dark roof,

the train talking with fuel.
Scythians poured wine over me.
They rolled up my shirt sleeve.

The wood is not the snow of March.
Gabriela shifts the documents.
The end is in the tree's hollow

as honey is in the tree's hollow.
Mount Kilimanjaro traveled like wire
around the bearded man when I

stripped the little horse's teeth.
A windowpane is weather and a bloom.
My blackbird is buckled. I feel your

dew, your head, with my fingers
I strew your hair. I break your neck
in the shrimp I eat. Ovid in his toga

agrees. My blackbird is an alloy of
buttonholes. The sea doesn't remain
on the tongue. I lick fins among

the duckling's toes. Beneath the lid is
alabaster. Seals hit me like
bingos.

Like wheat above the volcano.
Fall on your face.

Fall on your face.

The wheat is silk.
I do somersaults backwards,
I supply oxygen to the mountain.

Eat Adidas.
Eat eucalyptus hair.
Venus has three horns, cement and ether.

Load your hand.
I arrange limbs of the cuttlefish.
It has an invalid hand.

The first and third beech
trees are gutted by fire, and ivy
surrounds both of them as blues.

How Did I Feel on the Queen Mary?

Verena hit Bolkonski on the mouth
and *dai dai* also closed it. Snakes
bobbed *along* the technology.
A fish deceives the sea. The sea
pulls down. Wallets are foxes,
foxes lie in morgues. Whoever doesn't
have new shoes can join. The diminutive
of little fig is fig. A golden fleece
is a golden fleece. With years, mountains
adhere. Unsmooth them. A house, a toothpick,
a tank? A tarpaulin and a base for a tarpaulin.
Shove a dormouse cap on your head, and *along*. Now
as a ladder leaned on a wall: legs (the body)
boots (the body) a climbing spike (the body).

———

Woman and death are sisters.
Mother and death—sisters.
Man and death—brothers.
Father and death—brothers.
Man and death, two
giants,
two glittering spheres, two
lovers.
I—white alley—
both of them.

Tiepolo

I stood there in my khaki pants,
my teeth rending the curtain of time.

Fuck! Fuck! I said it with my open mouth,
screaming, all this with a purpose, that if they'd just
put the live hen in my mouth she wouldn't *thunder*.

Feathers in my mouth grow.

I dreamt Khlebnikov. He had the moist
snout of an animal which belonged to darkness.
I didn't see him. I was shocked by the smoothness,
the roundness and the grayness of his snout.

Hell Blau

The changing room lies in the courtyard.
There is the sea and the sack on the horizon.
In a few places, the sky is pierced with
the hell blue. The changing room
is covered, it's a little house.
The mango tree is hidden by fog.
The ferns grew like wheat.
The footprints in the woods are fresh.
The patriarch and his shadow,
the young patriarch with his hands
in his pocket comes closer to the angle
between lighted wall and dark wall.
There, nothing can be seen.
The flash is where the fog is set asunder.

Catalans, Moors

Poetry is a martyr's hatchery. A river
washes butter. *Warum Nichts?* A window
is put into a house, a house is put upon
the dawn. The clock strikes a quarter
of an hour. I'm left behind, I'm left behind,
I die as a crocodile at Menorca beach.
In the area of Ciutat (with the bike),
close to the young man in his twenties
bathing suit, reading Cavafi. Had he heavy
arms? Goran has heavy arms. I'm molasses,
don't forget. The cat with mottled
eyes. The voice met in the emptiness,
leading to the abyss. Burial grounds are
as at Potočka Zijalka. Strata on strata.

Faith

Precious copper mouth.
I hide, I hide my head in you.
I have only one white sense.
The rib from which Adam was made.

Cliffs, how they are spouting.
Azure, how it burns you.
Yours, sleepy and starving.
I am hugging you.

The Bone

Solemn is the fight,
wrinkled are the city
feathers.

Orpheus
bleeds from his mouth
and hair.

Marble soaked
a willow tree and then
the olive tree.

Newts had their eyes closed,
without yet having eyes. Štefka was
naked,

she breathed slowly,
the moonlight fell on her
and smelled of river

sand. They put
the helmet
made of

chains upon my head,
not to be bitten, pricked by
bees.

Buy Yourself a Bike, Breton Guy,
Buy Yourself a Bike!

Fays in the background are running short on linen.

Crumpled also is the eye of Pliny the Younger.

I live in leguminous plants as if in a castle.

I throw them away, not to burn my

bones. Xanadu is brown up to the elbows.

Would you see it? Would you interrogate it

if you saw it? The greatest hitchhike

happens in the night, while you sleep.

Lord, they strip my back. They dole

my skin among themselves, my upper lip gets

stronger. Always they use a clean clothespin,

especially for the story, asking me: after

your death will there be anybody to laugh?

Buy yourself a bike, Breton guy, buy yourself a bike!

IV

"The eyelash is an egg that has hatched too often. Now it is law
and law is the abyss cooped into the crab's illegible forehead."

—Michael Thomas Taren

Chariot of Fire

A bull's berry walks on a wire.
Windowpanes are mottled.
When water jets from a silver
teapot the giant throws a disk. It sizzles.
He turns his head.
His helmet touches the nib.

Sand and Rollerblades Two

In vertebra molluscs sour their
probationers. The eye links up and sinks.
The point is the only point, and prepared,

at the precise time it will be explained.
We will stand in a circle. The worms
will loosen the flesh, the one

who bends brassy hooks will come.
True, there'll be less camels than
two thousand years ago, but their tassels will

evaporate all the same. At Sinai one plays
bingo. I first hit yellow fish with a harpoon.
The cross is padded. The suffering

embraced the elegance of knuckles.
Beetles, if necessary, pee on a proboscis.
There's no end to it. Spring is everywhere.

There're floods, rolling whales, I found
a cranberry in the sand. I don't baffle you,
thorns simply stay in my head, my crown.

Mandelstam Dixit

Swahili is a cord on which a field poppy walks.
Eggs are fried straight into heaven's dew.
The spirit—disgusts.
Furled fingers—disgust.
The child's foot—bells toll,
the lass strikes into civilization.
I wanted to open the room but couldn't.
The moss had overgrown it.
A group of sheep and ducks climbed on the number
and hatched the core of the niche there.
The grandmother of living prose.
Yes, I open the umbrella because it rains.
Already I see the clear sky.
I pick the dandelion. In the rain I like it even better.

Sense of Hearing

The desire to be fast clones me.
How dark and heavy and silent is the bell.
Equal intervals calm down.
Why shouldn't I at last
say that I'm afraid of death.

Nobody Was Killed by the Blasts in the Night

A water lily keeps tolling: die the soul.
Cut off her little hands and lice.
Lie down in the breeding nest, in mother's

arms. Buy a sour cherry, buy a
sour cherry. No one who cleans, who
rules, who doesn't wear a helmet and

kills himself. Beneath the palm of your hand,
if you bite through your hand, it hurts.
Vesna will shine on the castle.

Cuk will get up from his gallows and meet
Javorsek. Four female screws lift up
the stone. Azure green baseball caps. I

climb the chair, hang the inscription.
Damp, putrid horse-hair's brood.
Turn around slowly and scream. What

about liqueurs? Yellow and black
inscriptions: West Coast Video. The snail
longs to somersault inside his house.

Washing in Gold

Dakhinis till and plow, drivel and
pry shingles from the roof.
The lump is microtone.
The windowpane vibrates when the steamship passes.

Isaac Luria did not like food.
He appreciated heavy components
of the dark meal like
hair and bonbons.
He smelled sweet, emptied himself, hugged.
He bowed down below the water, because he was singing.

Brahmins kept coming to get the seal.
Little does drank away layers of water.
Crickets even had extra buckets
on their backs, they watered themselves.

At times, from a clumsy cricket, a whole bucket
would roll away, with the sponge.
First the sponge swam in the water,
on the cricket's back below water.

The light and the light do not touch.
In between is the stomach of God, all squeezed.
He barely breathes, sets asunder, and sometimes, barely,
a butterfly's wing tickles him, touches him
when he begins to eat his own cocoon.

The Body and Sea Level

You sigh like bellows, but everyone already
fled the bellows. Lonely, tired, white hot
blaze of nothingness. Does a little straw,

arriving to such places, lick itself, does it
burn? Or perhaps greets, greets the red line before
burning it? What protected you? Were you wetted by

sponges? Did the whale reel his sea-factory,
all your life, around your head? And little
paws and red foxes which you took away?

You occupy too much space. Can you imagine
how much space, what kind of imprints,
what kind of wild rocks, canyons in the sand,

algae and shoes, huge amounts of mattresses
and people's shoes, all of which they allowed
to be flooded, would open for us? All air

below the surface was never flown across. And
if you'd lie on the stone with your paws pointing upwards,
your back would be on the stone for the first time,

the first time yellow forms in the air. You're like
an icebound skittle pin, *hot air,* you're lying, there are no
hills over the Loire, the rime deforms your mouth. Is it

that even my friends tell young poets I'm
dangerous? That they should watch out. That I'm
dangerous. That I'm a pagan priest. That I'm

objectively dangerous. That my character,
my goals, relative responsibility,

a bloodthirstily well-kept line between spirit and

flesh (experience) don't matter—it doesn't
change the fact that I'm dangerous. That I can
change entire nations in a wisp of straw.

———

The Last Judgment is bluish on the outside and
                                crisscrossed with veins.
In 1939 Simone Weil goes to Solemnes for
                                the Easter holiday.
In 1963 Braque dies.

Spring Street

I had a sweet liver. Coasts to the sky.
Honking of the truck on Houston Street,
the dark one.

The tribe demolished the layer cake.
The layer cake destroyed the seed.
Salt. Midgets. I bite your white, white bridge.

You sleepy, softly turning wheel.
As a winch pulling a boat to earth,
you lift, you wreck my veins.

Let it flow into you, let it flow into you, my sweet juice.
You need me. If not, you wouldn't tear me apart.
You wouldn't move your warm

bread, wrapped in rags.
For you yourself are pinned together, for me you crunch.
The sea of blood is not aware of the heat of your heart.

And cunning. But you don't know how
rich. Carried toward your bite mark.
Spend. You froth, you froth,

red blood breaks into a waterfall.
O leaf of my tree,
white fire of my grief.

You are seized, my son, you are seized.
You flow away on the path
from which you came.

Monstrum (Lat.) from the Verb
Monstrare

I add to the story, because no doubt
there will be many theses on
who I am. My life is clear the way
my books are clear. I am
as alone as you, voyeur. Like you
I flinch if someone sees me.
I look into your eyes. We both know
the question. Who kills? Who stays?
Who watches? The one furiously
taking his clothes off to be innocent,
isn't that a mask? Your heart beats
because your blood beats. You have
the same right as I do, I, who am
your guardian angel, your monster.

Sun That Heats the Other Sun

Goddess who took me
and dispersed me as powdery snow,
ate me as an apple and
forged me in the tree,
stop!
Kill somewhere else. I
regret. Do you hear me,
I regret now, I regret!

O, if I didn't take the first bait,
a tiny white blaze
whose half-awake fang I've
crushed to stir my blood.
Epileptic fit! How you
poisoned me with your skin,
with your glitter pouring into
a rage,
with pistachio nuts that, as
an athlete, I milled to be
everything, like a joke,
like an addition to life.

I will lose my mind.
I can't endure this white
chain crushing my knees,
the sinusoids smacking like
Hottentots, not giving a damn
about the cut.

Petals grind my ship.
I'll cut off my prick.
With my licked fingers I can

no longer rest on
your belly's membrane.
I can no longer determine sunrises.
A flock tumbled over me,
the waterfall carries me away.
My mind burns.

O, where is the
white golden deer running
wild because of my scent,
knelt and breathing
musk in my eyes until I gave
birth to a crystal.
Once I was the destiny,
now I'm a wound.

My palm poisoned all living waters,
me, who is your
orgasm, white beauty.
My mind is cardboard,
you, who are nothing, whose paw was
hidden in joy and
a hurricane that resembles a
small sunny bird.

Poem

Where am I?
Where do my gallows stand?
Why do I have granulated eyes?
The town will follow you.

The crocodile stuffs my body into its tongue.
What sense does it make to be left without
sadness, in the middle of these artificial fires?
I vomit because I have no more

sadness. I have no
                    rest. I don't
caress your little body, Metka.
You're far away and the language is near.
It picks me from the herd and eats me.

It rolls on me like Hannibal with his donkeys,
already I stressed his elephants too much,
I hope he had donkeys too.
My poetry is no longer credible,
not for a long time.

It rots from the sheer glowing.

Abraham Abulafia

Do you conspire?
I drop leaves.
From the elephant, the cigarette butt falls ill.

There are records in your house,
nobody will eat them.

My cousin wears a wide silk skirt.
When the horse touches it with its horseshoe,
sparks glitter.

———

The hand is the hand of Athens and Rome.

———

Spaniards are unbound by hayracks.
The circle is von Mally in the sun.

———

The bird chokes the pond.
Music, music, music bruises.
The swamp in the mirror is moist.
On the bunch of flowers there's a nose, no *flowers*.
The Vardar river, unflushed, like immaculate white
jackets.

———

The contour breaks the letter to the neck.
The contour breaks the fleet to the neck.
The contour, on moist grass, calms the gathered crowd.
The wheat hires itself out to the pasha.

———

My sweetheart,
how are you, my dove?

———

The hill, wrapped into the soliloquy, lacerates the lump of meat.
The legs are shades of black harvest, there're no arms.
Vertebralicarity?
Heraclitus in the nut that I hold in my fist.

———

Sing:
the bag,
the bag,
where are you leaving me the night?
Where do you gather the sticks of glory,
that the turpentine starts to smell?

Sing!

———

Two people jumping in their mouths,
on the drawn mesh, will tear themselves apart.
As the beech mast divides.

A complicated heavy sin.
A complicated heavy grail.

———

The number of velvet is velvety porcelain.
The female key, the gemantry.

Memory Tugs the Arm

No diary. No wires. No splashing.
When you take a newborn from a bathtub,
he watches, he doesn't bathe, you roll

his little body in the light, gray-green towel.
Or do you only blot him? It's no good to think.
Whales open their day planners on the Atlantic.

Do they bind feet and veins? There was no glass.
Before there was glass, there was alabaster.
Saints, lined up, as if under a kind of soap.

The sky had to pant and pant. On the third
fifth of the bridge toward Vendée it pierced
through the clouds. Not only. In the form

of the sun. Not as the sun. As its light.
And this one only reflects, glittering
on the upper epidermis of the Loire surface,

in the space that flared up. It differentiates
between the first and the second,
also between the seventh, eighth

and ninth girders. I saw it and typed it up.
As if I'd play with a rein. As if I'd carry
the late-twentieth century technological

achievement—transversally—hide
diamonds, hide cranberries, hide an inured position.
How to wake up the horse from the golden

carriage, my eyes oriented toward
the East. I strew no peas on the steamers.
Light flares up by itself, when it wishes.

Sisters

Rub your seed into the child's mouth.
He is tepid.
Caress his brain's palm.
His skin splits, like sausage
skin in splitting.
Strasbourg spouts, jona,
calm measure.
Rub your seed into the child's mouth.
Don't be afraid. I'm not scared anymore.
Mercy is made of small blue
balls and our palate is among them.
In my hand,
in your thunder, I wander.

I Ask Myself If Fitzko Knows Cold Too

In the open air purses melt.

Many birds know cold, not me.

The story plunged into the mud.
I rutted a targa.
No meat here.

Who will read, who will read, one for sure.

One will read and save humanity.

Blacks are the greatest mother's little souls.

I believe in the pit, up to Carpathians.

All tenants of the floor above me at
28 Masarykova were cold.

To Piranesi on My Visit to L.A.

A damp, huge bat. At first I didn't even notice it
above the eternal city. A wet loaf of bread
in the ground plan, a monster, you've made a glass

out of the sky. You want to show your veins, your
pulse, your bulges, the place where your machines
rattle beneath engines. Where the skin comes

rushing from fountains, with traps for bumblebees,
with a sinkhole for sheep. A sheep rises to
graze and disappears, Aldo Moro disappears.

On the fringe, yes, but in the range of your huge
canvas covers. The ground plans smelled of mafia,
rivers were full of ink. Sant Angelo in Trastevere,

little trains at different times. Even then they were
already selling mothers, mushrooms, slippers,
directly from the apartment. Do you remember

how you were the first to rage on Monte Pincio, not
even noticing that you didn't make it? Gober sent you
an apron. In a little California stall, with artificial

waters, waterwomen, crabs, a thin plate, little grass
and curs, not to forget the hungry milk of airplanes,
a folded aluminum tube. Where did you throw your

cigarette butt? In your own brook, under your little
stall, under your parquet floor? Frey with his theatre, with
his flood and his tongue, had more magic. Also,

with how he used his binoculars. Also, when
actors didn't start swimming. We started to dance
immediately. Lynn screamed. Fred, rolling his

sleeves, didn't believe her. But mainly, with a blast
of our pace, we shot down that huge, plush
corpse in the shape of the cloud above the eternal city.

To Reap the Field

There's still space for a golden door,
there's still space for the darkness of a prince.
Flashes of crystals, unite.
Break the arch.

There are still crenels, the crenels,
the crenels under the linden tree,
in the crenel under the linden tree there are black ships.
Still the waves break like whispering,
in the wings they imprint themselves
like rum, like triumph.

19. IX. 1982

I opened the fig and in it
squatted an angel, bound with his own hair.
Axes threatened his honey,
I tore his eye though it hurt him.
Out of the red forest a deer sprang.
He came close to the angel, close with his snout,
and disappeared. Like a dark papyrus
a mass showed behind the crown
and started to spin.
O the name!
Ireneus, Elephant, Milčin, Wedding Guest, Parnassus,
Geza, Ahmed, Blood, Deer, Tempest
intertwined like roots and grew,
and kept shooting the folding fan of crosses
until they undulated like medusa's whips
in the lazy, agitated sea.

Let the tree have a blue heart.
Let's open the house windows around the blue heart!
Let's lure the sun into the windowpanes!
Let's hear the blue blast in the tooth,
let it resound, hollow inside the water.
The fig: the temple and the tempest,
the power which holds together the crown of Christ.

O climb, climb!
And he tore himself away like a cocoon.
With his palm he clung to my white neck,
because his body flew
much faster than mine.
But mine was larger and heavier, more guided

and it curtained the horizon.
We made a suitcase. From a shawl we made a bundle,
from a bundle a pueblo.

Eyes, a nose, a mouth, caves for ears.
First the city was built, then the man.
At first the city had more flesh than the man.
Give it back to him.
Give it back to him, I tell you.
So that the beak doesn't entangle itself in the moss,
so that the crown doesn't explode because of the horrible
pressure.
Or take the machine and make the nib,
just as the ice-cream man makes the nib.
And this wish: the arch above the circle is heaven.
The blind window of the world.

Flower

We are the people. Rose and wound.
Flower. Make spring thick for me too.

Acknowledgments

My deepest gratitude goes to the people and institutions that made me happy writing: heartfelt thanks to Lynn Emanuel, who invited me to the University of Pittsburgh; to my two former students, Thomas Kane, who with enormous patience survived my constant changes while we were translating, and Michael Thomas Taren, who allowed me to steal the title of this book from a line of his manuscript; to the Bogliasco Foundation; to the Civitella Ranieri Foundation; and to the following publications, in which these poems first appeared:

The American Poetry Review: "Now Karen and Richard's House," "Nice Hat. Thanks.," "Washing in Gold"
The Antioch Review: "Hell Blau," "Sisters"
Blackbird: "Faith"
Black Warrior: "Monstrum . . . "
Boston Review: "To Reap the Field"
Chicago Review: "Benito Mussolini Has His Fingers in His Pants," "Buy Yourself a Bike, Breton Guy, Buy Yourself a Bike!," "Beauty of Man," "Amtrak, New York—Montreal, January 24, 1974," "I Ask Myself If Fitzko Knows Cold Too," "The Little Plaque Is Formed by Fire and God"
Colorado Review: "Sardines," "Moro," "The deer . . .," "Virgil"
Conduit: "You *are* my angel.," "Woman and Death"
Crazy Horse: "Dark Glasses," "Flowers"
Denver Quarterly: "Are More Mysterious than My Rain," "How the Hills"
European Judaism: "Abraham Abluafia"
Good Foot: "Mangalia"
Grand Street: "Who lives in the error . . . "; "Mountains, all their life . . . "
Gulf Coast: "Nobody Was Killed by the Blasts in the Night"
Handsome: "Zebra's Body"
Harp and Altar: "Memory Tugs the Arm"

Hunger Mountain: "Black Sun"

Iowa Review: "These Are the Islands"

Jubilat: "Blossom and Blood"

Lyric: "Eternity"

Melancholia Tremulous Dreadlocks: "Leonardo's Horse"

New American Writing: "Afternoon, at the Table, above the Underworld"

The Ninth Letter: "The Shirt"

Octopus: "Chariot of Fire"

Orient Express: "How the Hills"

Parthenon West: "The Right of the Elephant's Bone"

PEN: "Frontier"

Poetry Inhalation: "The Body of Giordano Bruno"

Poetry London: "Monstrum . . . "

Pleiades: "Green Catastrophe in Trieste, 1910"

Pretext: "You *are* my angel."

Public Space: "The Detour Across Deleware"

Verse: "Sand and Rollerblades," "Sand and Rollerblades Two"

Whisky and For: "Madreperla, Gifted to the Scythians"

"The deer . . . " was published as a limited edition broadside by Empyrean Press

Translator Index

Memory Tugs the Arm—*poet and Thomas Kane*
Monstrum (Lat.) from the Verb *Monstrare*—*poet and Phillis Levin*
Moro—*poet and Thomas Kane*
Mountains, all their life . . . —*poet and Phillis Levin*
Movements—*poet and Thomas Kane*
My Brides Are of Gobelin—*poet and Thomas Kane*
Nakedness of the Wall—*poet and Thomas Kane*
New Moon—*poet and Thomas Kane*
Nice Hat. Thanks.*—*poet and Thomas Kane*
Nobody Was Killed by the Blasts in the Night—*poet and Thomas Kane*
Now Karen and Richard's House—*poet and Thomas Kane*
Piece of Earwig, Fainted in Amber, Can Plug the Crime Out, The—*poet and Thomas Kane*
Poem—*poet and Thomas Kane*
Right of the Elephant's Bone, The—*poet and Thomas Kane*
Sand and Rollerblades—*poet and Peter Richards*
Sand and Rollerblades Two—*poet and Peter Richards*
Sardines—*poet and Thomas Kane*
Sense of Hearing—*poet and Thomas Kane*
Shirt, The—*poet and Peter Richards*
Sisters—*Brian Henry*
Spring Street—*poet and Joshua Beckman*
Sun That Heats the Other Sun—*poet and Peter Richards*
Suns, The—*poet and Thomas Kane*
Sword, The—*poet and Matthew Rohrer*
The deer braids . . . —*poet and Christopher Merrill*
The Last Judgment . . . —*poet and Phillis Levin*
These Are the Islands—*Peter Richards and Ana Jelnikar*
Three Flies—*poet and Thomas Kane*
Tiepolo—*poet and Thomas Kane*
To Piranesi on My Visit to L.A.—*poet and Thomas Kane*
To Reap the Field—*poet and Peter Richards*
To Świetlicki—*poet and Thomas Kane*
Virgil—*poet and Thomas Kane*
Warning the Sphinx—*poet and Thomas Kane*
Washing in Gold—*poet and Thomas Kane*
Who Is Berkopec—*poet and Thomas Kane*
Who lives in the error . . . —*poet and Phillis Levin*
Will You Die?—*poet and Thomas Kane*
Woman and Death . . . —*poet and Matthew Rohrer*
You *are* my angel . . . —*poet and Joshua Beckman*
You did not snow . . . —*poet and Matthew Rohrer*
you'll be surprised . . . —*poet and Anselm Hollo*
Zebra's Body—*poet and Thomas Kane*

* "Nice Hat. Thanks." is the title of Joshua Beckman and Matthew
  Rohrer's book of poems